The **ENGLISH** *COLLECTION*

WRITING
FOR
CHILDREN

Brenda Pinder

LONGMAN

CONTENTS

6 Information for children   30

7 Mounting a campaign   36

8 Have you got it right?   41

9 Final project – a magazine for young people   45

To the pupil:

This series is for your pleasure and your profit. It's like a do-it-yourself kit – but with clear instructions.

Our main hope for the series is that you enjoy doing the reading, writing, talking and listening it involves. This has been an important consideration in choosing material. But, of course, we also need to help you fulfil the requirements of GCSE and the National Curriculum. The range of work will give you opportunities to develop your ability in every aspect of English, including assessment of your own progress – watch for the 'Look Back' headings in each section.

We want you to make – to create for yourself –
    stories
    poems
    advertisements
    magazine articles
    letters
    plays –
a full variety of styles of writing.

Each book in this series takes you carefully through the creation process, working individually, in small groups or as a complete class, helping you to –
    prepare
    discuss
    develop ideas
    plan
    redraft –
so that your final pieces are presented with clarity and care.

At the same time, you will be showing your ability to read –
    fiction
    non-fiction
    between the lines
    with discrimination
    aloud or silently.

You will be talking to different people in different situations –
    your classmates
    your teachers
    members of your community.

You will show that you understand that speech varies with context, and that you can listen sensitively and with comprehension to a variety of people.

READING, WRITING, SPEAKING and LISTENING – these are the three main aspects of the National Curriculum. The English Collection will help you make the most of your ability in each of them.

indicates a piece of writing

indicates oral work

Programmes of Study in Key Stage 4 that are covered in *Writing for Children*

Speaking and listening

Pupils should be given opportunities to:

- express and justify feelings, opinions and viewpoints with increasing sophistication
- discuss increasingly complex issues
- recount events and narrate stories
- assess and interpret arguments and opinions with increasing precision and discrimination
- present ideas, experiences and understanding in a widening range of contexts and with an increasing awareness of audience and purpose
- respond to increasingly complex instructions and questions
- present factual information in a clear and logical manner
- discuss issues in small and large groups, taking account of the views of others and negotiating a consensus
- report and summarise in a range of contexts
- talk about stories, poems, playscripts and other texts

Reading

Pupils should be given opportunities to:

- read a variety of genres, including pre-twentieth century literature
- handle a range of information texts in a variety of media
- find and select information for themselves and use it effectively

Writing

Pupils should be given opportunities to:

- control the subject and organisation of different types of text
- match form to subject matter and readership
- develop an understanding of the range of purposes which written language serves
- draft, revise and proofread their work
- write in a range of forms
- write for a range of purposes including describing, explaining, giving instructions, reporting, expressing a point of view
- write in aesthetic and imaginative ways
- organise and express their meaning appropriately for a specific audience

1

YOUR AUDIENCE

—

This book will start you off on writing for a very different audience from the one you usually address in your GCSE folder – the teacher or the examiner; different also from writing for yourself. You are going to be writing for a specific audience – younger children. To make a success of it you will need to consider just *how* writing for them will have to be different – in content, language and presentation.

How children use language

Here are some pieces that young children themselves have written, which will give you some insight into the way they use language.

Jennifer

My Rabbit Always
Away in the
Runs
gorben

Mrs Barwells House

Mrs Barwells house was once a shop that sold clothes like bonnets, dresses, hats and underware. It was our by a J. CATT about eighty years ago. We looked around the garden to see if we could find any traces of the old metal fence and patio. First of all we found some of the metal railings which was the fence. We also looked in the grass to see if we could see if there was signs that a path had been there. We saw where the path was because it was not growing as good as the rest of the path. Then we looked at the photo and saw that the big front window had been knocked down and leveled some it was level with the walls. When we looked closely we saw that the bricks and cement was newer. Mrs Barwell showed us inside the house to show us where they used to store every thing. She showed us a door that been blocked in. They had quite a new extension built on the side of the house. We were comparing the house like it is now to an old photo taken in 1910.

On Sunday I went to the sea-side to swim my dad want to swim too mum is eating an apple at the sea-side and I just swim.

Stephen

At christmas time we have carl singers and there sing carls abwat babuy jeses and remid us of hem and we have christmas trees

Fireworks (Sarah-Jane)

5.10.90   Fireworks.

I stand in the dark cold night.

Wating for the fireworks to come.

Suddenly a deafening bang souns.

Bright gliterig colours spurting out of

the sky.

pinks blues yellows golds and greens.

More bangs.

more colours.

I am paralysed.

Iluminous greens.

Iluminous pinks and golds.

There is a silence

The fire works have dissaperd.

No more fireworks till next year

                                                                    Sarah-Jane

My pets (Claire)

My   pets.   claire

I have to dogs to cats and one fish.
The fish is my brothers and The cat and
dogs are my mums and my dads and Iains
and I. one day my big dog Amy went
out side to play with Iain and I. Then
Iain and I went in our house and Amy
played out side. when Iain went out
side to get Amy she had goon Iain came
back in side and told my mum and Dad.
My mum and dad looked in the back garges
and in the house for Amy then the
front door bell rang and my dad when
to open it when he opened the door
there was a man and Amy. my dad
said Thank you very much and closed
the door. My dad said not to do that
agan to Amy. And Amy whent to bed.

▥ How old do you think the children were when they wrote these pieces? Working with a partner, try to put them into age order, from youngest to oldest. Remember that handwriting may give you a clue, but it could prove an unreliable test unless it is backed up by evidence in content or vocabulary. You have only to look around at your own class to see how hard it is to judge maturity on handwriting alone! Try to find evidence from the pieces as to why you decide on a certain order; make some rough notes of your reasons.

▥ Then compare notes with the rest of the group in discussion.

How adults write for very young children

☞ In pairs, take it in turns to read the following four extracts (here and on the top of page 10). Three of these have been written for very young children. One of the pieces has *not* been written for young children. Which one? How can you tell?

Reading Scheme

Here is Peter. Here is Jane. They like fun.
Jane has a big doll. Peter has a ball.
Look, Jane, look! Look at the dog! See him run!

Here is Mummy. She has baked a bun.
Here is the milkman. He has come to call.
Here is Peter. Here is Jane. They like fun.

Go Peter! Go Jane! Come, milkman, come!
The milkman likes Mummy. She likes them all.
Look, Jane, look! Look at the dog! See him run!

Here are the curtains. They shut out the sun.
Let us peep! On tiptoe Jane! You are small!
Here is Peter. Here is Jane. They like fun.

I hear a car, Jane. The milkman looks glum.
Here is Daddy in his car. Daddy is tall.
Look, Jane, look! Look at the dog! See him run!

Daddy looks very cross. Has he a gun?
Up milkman! Up milkman! Over the wall!
Here is Peter. Here is Jane. They like fun.
Look Jane, look! Look at the dog! See him run!

Wendy Cope

"Go home," said the hens.
"No," said little pig.

"Go home," said the ducks.
"No," said little pig.

"Go home," said the cows.
"No," said little pig.

"Go home," said the sheep.
"No," said little pig.

"Go home," said the butcher,
"or I'll make you into sausages."

They go along a country road,
Ticketty-tat, ticketty-tat.
They go along a country road,
Tina and Jessie and Cat.

They come into a station,
Ticketty-tat, ticketty-tat.
They come into a station,
Tina and Jessie and Cat.

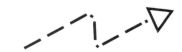

What's in the hutch, Spot?

✎ Look at the three extracts that have been written for children. Again, see if you can decide what age group each is aimed at. They are from books used to teach children to read; does this make it easier to decide the age group? Reading Schemes, still used in some primary schools, are very systematic in introducing and repeating certain groups of words; perhaps you can remember these from *your* early reading experience?

How did you decide on age groups? You will probably agree that the following factors influenced you:

1 repetition of words and phrases;
2 length of sentences;
3 difficulty of vocabulary.

What about the subject matter? These examples were too short for you to notice much about that, but, from your own experience, do you think there are certain topics and themes which especially interest certain age groups? Talk about this for a little while with your partner, drawing on your combined knowledge of younger brothers and sisters and your own memories.

LOOK BACK

On your own, make some notes summarising what you have concluded about the differences of writing for children and for adults. You will need to refer to these from time to time while you write.

VOICES FROM THE PAST

—

Before looking closely at various ways of writing for children in our own time, it will be interesting to see what previous ages thought was suitable writing for children.

OF PICTURES AND STORIES.   17

ENTICING TO EVIL.

THE wise man says, "If sinners entice thee, consent thou not."

To *entice*, here means, as most of our youngest readers know, to try to lead one to do wrong. Whenever one child tries to induce another to do any thing that is sinful, or in any way improper, that child is *enticing* the other. And in all such cases the exhortation is, "*Consent thou not.*"

Our fine picture gives us an example of *enticing to evil*. Here are two school-girls. We will call them

2

18   THE CHILDREN'S ALBUM

Sarah and Ellen. They are just out of school. You can see the low country schoolhouse back of them, near by. They have seated themselves under those large trees; and Ellen is on her knees, trying to coax Sarah to do something that is wrong. She is *enticing* her. Perhaps she is trying to get her to stay out of school, to run away from home, to go off with her berrying, or something of the kind.

She doesn't look like a *wicked* girl. But you can not always tell the state of the heart by the looks. *Satan* sometimes, when he wishes to entice people, puts on the appearance of an *angel of light*. He does it on purpose to deceive. So Ellen has put on that pleasant, winning countenance, that she may deceive Sarah, and more easily lead her to yield to her wishes.

Sarah seems to feel that all is not right. She looks down at her books, doubtful, and rather sad. Perhaps she *knows* that Ellen is enticing her to what is wrong, and she is questioning with herself whether she shall yield to her enticement.

Do you think she will yield? Will she forget all her kind mother's warnings and exhortations, and the wishes of her teacher, and disregard the reproving voice of her conscience, and yield? We shall have to leave her here, with her sad looks, undecided. But let us all *hope* she will remember the words of the wise man, and *consent not*.

Little friend, what would you do if in her place? Do you say, "*I* would not consent"?

Well, remember that when next *enticed* to evil.

From *The Children's Album*, an illustrated book of instruction for children, published in 1869.

Discuss the writer's purpose here.

How do you think a child today would react to this? Which ideas and words would you not find in a modern children's book? Why not?

THE INFANT'S GRAMMAR.

THE ADVERBS.

And these had attendants, called ADVERBS by name:

To teach the Verbs proper behaviour they came.

They told them how they might more GRACEFULLY dance,

More QUICKLY might run, or more MERRILY prance;

They rous'd those that LAZILY slept on the floor,

Made others, more MANNERLY, move from the door;

And told how they YESTERDAY languish'd in sorrow,

Though so merry TO-DAY, and might still be TOMORROW.

From a book published in 1824.

This is intended to inform in an interesting way. What does the presentation of the information tell you about the teaching of grammar in the nineteenth century?

It is needless to go into questions of feeding or manage-ment, as we assume this pet to be used as a companion. A fox-terrier or other dog of the same size will thrive very well on scraps from the table. He should be kept clean, but this does not signify that he needs the washing required amid the smoke and grime of a town, or even much brushing, if he has an abundance of out-of-door exercise. It may be necessary to dust him with insect powder occasionally, though few dogs are infested with parasites of which they cannot get rid by their own efforts; and any dealer in canine necessaries will give you something to reduce that strong effluence of dog which comes from some more than others. After that he may be kept in the house, and sleep on the rug in your bedroom.

Ordinary common sense will tell you that boys occasionally treat dogs rather thoughtlessly, as when one is allowed to fetch and carry stones, or tempted to go into the water oftener than is desirable. The dog should be a companion and playfel-low, and be invariably treated with sense and consideration.

From *Country Pastimes for Boys* published in 1895.

In this extract language, presentation and even content are very different from what they would be today. Make notes on how you would set out a piece advising a child how to care for a dog, today.

Now I want you for a few moments to think very hard about yourself and when you come to think of it you are a very remarkable person. You have a body which is quite the most remarkable thing in the world. It is not like the chair which you are sitting on – a heavy, lifeless thing. It is alive – very wonderfully alive. If you could see inside it you would find the most wonderful system of tubes and muscles and bones all with a special and very carefully planned work to do. Smaller than these and to be seen only through a microscope are millions and millions of tiny cells, tiny things with all kinds of queer shapes, but every one of them very much alive and with carefully planned work to do. Of course you have heard all that before, but have you ever seriously sat down for a few minutes and thought about it? Have you ever thought about it so long that at the end of it you said to yourself 'What a very wonderful thing *I* am.' If not, please do so now. It won't take you very long to feel like that. Think of your eyes – and all that they can do. Close them for thirty seconds and miss them for a little while, then open them again and see what a difference it makes. I once knew a man who collected lots of money for the blind by that little experiment.

From *The Golden Pathway Treasury of Knowledge*, published in the 1930s. The writer goes on to discuss the importance of the mind and the need to go to school to develop it.

◿▷ One of you read this (in a solemn voice) to a partner or the rest of the class. In what ways does the piece seem 'dated'? Consider not only what is said, but also the language used.

What are the differences?

None of these pieces would find a place in a modern children's book.
◿▷ Write a paragraph explaining why not. This will help you to see what is important about writing for children today. Consider content and purpose, language and presentation.

Little adults

This portrait photograph gives us an insight into the attitudes towards children at the time it was taken: they were dressed as little adults and were treated as little adults. Very few concessions were made in their books to their inexperience and limited vocabulary. No doubt with lots of children this worked very well: a lot was expected and a wide vocabulary and fluent style quickly absorbed. But how many fell by the wayside and never found the pleasure that books can offer? Few people today would advocate a return to this kind of writing for children.

So your approach will have to be a bit more in keeping with the interests and abilities of your chosen audience.

3

TELL ME A STORY

—

'I didn't know you could read,' said Granny.
'C-A-T,' William spelled out.
'What does that say?' asked Granny.
'Wheelbarrow,' said William.

Early stories are told mainly through pictures –
and so are many later ones, though we call
them 'cartoons'. This section looks at ways to
tell a story that do not rely mainly on the
written word.

Picture book for the under fives

Can you remember the very first books you ever
had read to you? They have a way of staying in
the mind for a very long time and even old
people can sometimes recall in great detail their
first books. Perhaps it is because young children
love repetition and always seem to want the
same ones read over and over again, until they
can almost recite them by heart.

The ingredients of a good picture book

What does a good picture book need? Discuss with a partner what you would expect would make a good 'buy' for an under-five. Remember it will have to be read by an adult, so maybe it needs to have some appeal for parents as well. Jot down what you both think are the necessary ingredients. Should it:

- be colourful?
- have a high proportion of pictures to text?
- have large printing?
- start the child on the learning to read process?
- be funny?

Try to have a look at a few books designed for the under-fives. The local bookshop will have a selection, as well as the childrens' section of the local library and, if your school runs a child care course, there are sure to be some examples there that you could ask to see.

Using all the information you have gained, try your hand at a Picture Book yourself. Keep the storyline simple, illustrate it with colourful pictures (cut out of magazines, if you don't have much artistic talent) and plan carefully how much of the story is to go on each page before you begin. It doesn't have to be large: children also like miniature books. If you can't think up an original story, use a traditional fairy tale, in your own words, but keep in mind throughout the audience for which you are writing.

A copy of your book can go into your folder, with an explanation of what you set out to do, but it would also be good to send the stories to a local playgroup, if this is possible.

This is a picture book very popular with the first year students at Infants Schools. Why do you think the children like this particular book?

The big skeleton and the little skeleton played on the swings.
They threw a stick for the dog.

Suddenly something happened.
The dog skeleton chased the stick,
tripped over a park bench,
bumped into a tree –

WOOF!

Cartoons

It is not only children who enjoy stories told in cartoon form. Many adults turn to the comic strips in their daily newspaper before going on to read anything else. Do you have a favourite cartoon character you always look for in the paper?

Visualising the joke

Discuss this example of a popular cartoon with a partner. The cartoon does not use many words and the drawings help to visualise the joke. Try to work out what the joke would look like in words alone. It will probably end up pretty longwinded and not nearly as effective.

Find a joke, suitable for primary school children, which could be told in cartoon form and present it in six or eight frames. It doesn't matter if you can't draw: stick people and animals will do just as well. What is important is to plan your story so that it fits exactly into the chosen number of frames. You'll find it easier if you sketch out the first and the last, and then decide on the stages in between. It is a useful exercise in thinking ahead and planning a story. You may have already done something like this in storyboard form.

Keep words to a minimum: you might even be able to do without them altogether. If you need speech or thoughts, use balloons; or you could have a short sentence under each picture.

When you have finished this planning process, divide your page into the correct number of frames and make your final version.

Just in case you can't find any suitable jokes, here are a couple that might be suitable:

One Squadron-Leader who had just been promoted to Group-Captain was bursting with pride at his up-grading. He was sitting in his new office when there came a knock on the door.

'Come in!' he called, and as the door opened he picked up his phone and said, 'Very well, Air Marshal. Thank you, Air Marshal. Goodbye.'

He put down the receiver and said to the air-man who had just entered, 'Well, what is it?'

And the airman replied, 'I've just come to reconnect your phone, sir.'

The harpsichordist had a theory that music soothed the wildest of animals. So he trekked to the middle of the African jungle, taking his harpsichord with him. All round were the roars and screams of ferocious animals.

When he started to play, the roars died down and a strange hush fell on the jungle. One by one the animals came out to listen, sitting quietly in a circle . . . an elephant, a buffalo, a gorilla, a crocodile, a gigantic snake. Suddenly, with an ear-splitting roar, a lion leapt from the jungle and bit off the harpsichordist's head. The other animals were a-ghast.

'Why the heck did you do that?' trumpeted the elephant. 'For the first time in our lives we've heard beautiful music. Now you've gone and ruined everything. Why did you do it?'

'Eh?' said the lion, cupping a paw to his ear, 'what did you say?'

Share your cartoons by passing them round or displaying them. It might even be possible to photocopy them and staple them together as a book for a local primary school.

Cartoons can also be serious

The technique of cartoon making is not confined to humorous subjects. You may know the cartoon story by Raymond Briggs, called *When the Wind Blows*, which is about a nuclear war. The impact of the 'joky' presentation of such a terrifying subject is enormous. There are also cartoon versions of some of Shakespeare's plays which use the actual words of the characters but by the drawings attempt to make the storyline easier to follow.

Try taking a well known fairytale and retelling it in cartoon form. Alternatively, write your own story for six to seven year olds and present it as a cartoon.

LOOK BACK

Try your cartoons out on your friends, and, if possible, a younger brother or sister, or a child next door. Get some feedback about how easy or difficult it was to follow the storyline.
Finish off your unit for your folder by adding your own criticisms of your efforts.

The Magic Box

Once upon a time, far away in China, there lived a wise old mandarin, who was well known for his priceless collection of antique vases. He found that his precious pieces of porcelain were gradually disappearing and he knew that the only people who had access to his private apartments where they were kept were his personal servants. So he called them together and questioned them, but they all denied knowledge of the thefts.

He thought up a clever plan to find the culprit: he produced a large black lacquered box, which he told them all was a magic box which could detect lies. If anyone were to tell a lie while his hand were inside the box, it would magically snap shut and chop the offender's hand off. He then instructed each of them to go, one at a time, behind a screen, to put his right hand into the box's opening and swear solemnly that he had not stolen the vases.

Each one obeyed and swore what was required and the box did not snap shut. So then the Mandarin made them all line up in front of him and show their right hands. All but one were stained with black, and this one he accused and dismissed. He had covered the inside of the box with stove blacking and the only one afraid to put his hand inside it was clearly guilty.

This story has a number of ingredients that would appeal to children – some suspense, a sense of justice, and a hint of magic (though this turns out in the end to be a trick).

Only the bare bones of the story are told here: we aren't told how many servants there were; we don't know anything else about them apart from the fact that one is a thief. The mandarin himself is given some sort of character (i.e. he is wise) but there are no real individuals in the story. So there are lots of extra details that could be added to the tale. The central plot could even be transferred into a totally different setting – say, the Godfather of a Chicago gang who uses a 'lie detector' to find his thief.

Turning the story into a play

⟿ Work in groups for this activity and devise your own way of telling this tale to children of about eight or nine years of age, by means of some sort of drama. You could turn it into a play in a couple of scenes, or you could use a storyteller who introduces the characters at the beginning and links up the action between scenes. You could even tell it entirely in mime while the narrator reads the story. You may wish to keep the Chinese setting and could think up ways of suggesting this in how the story is presented.

You may change any details you like as long as the result is still likely to appeal to the given age group. Add further details as you wish, and expand on the characters in any way you care to.

Rehearse your improvisation and share it with the rest of the class. The final performance should be to a primary school class, or to the youngest children in your own school, if this could be arranged.

⟿ Alternatively, you could make the story into a radio play and tape it, to be played to an audience of primary school children. This would mean you would be working entirely in the medium of sound. You would probably need a narrator and some improvised special effects.

4

WRITING FICTION FOR CHILDREN

—

If you are going to write successfully for children, you need to find out what they enjoy reading, at different age levels. In this section, you will be finding out what a well-known writer has to say about writing for children. Then you will be researching the kind of books that are popular with the age group you have chosen and writing your own story for that particular group.

An interview with Jan Mark

Jan Mark has written for a wide range of age groups – ranging from *Nothing To Be Afraid Of* for young children, *Thunder and Lightnings* for the eight to twelve year olds, to *The Ennead* for young adults.

This is what she had to say about her writing:

I started my career as a children's writer by entering a Penguin Books Competition in the *Guardian* newspaper – open only to writers who had never had a children's book published before. The prize, which I won, was publication, and the book was *Thunder and Lightnings*.

Publishers always seem to want books for this age group; it seems to be the hardest market to supply, for some reason, but I personally prefer writing for older children and young adults because it opens up so many more possible topics. Short stories are perhaps the most satisfying of all as they can be enjoyed by all age groups, right up to adult. The books I've been most proud of are *Divide and Rule*, *Aquarius* and *The Ennead* – all with science fiction or historical backgrounds, so I can invent my own environment – and these aren't really children's books at all. Even when I write for a young audience, I never write down to my readers and don't consciously adapt my language. But I always use a good deal of dialogue and this will reflect the age of the characters who are speaking.

I don't think there's any fundamental difference between writing for children and for adults – I just write stories for READERS and can't always predict who will enjoy reading them. If I'm working on a book for very young children I also have to think about making it interesting for grown-ups too; after all, the adults will be the ones who will have to read it aloud!

A great deal of hard work goes into a typical novel. Writing isn't, and shouldn't be, easy. Each of my books represents at least six months hard work and at least three drafts. I pause between each of these for at least a few days, so I can look at what I've done with fresh eyes. I don't have any theory of writing except to get something – anything – down on paper. That's the most useful advice I can offer you about writing: it's no use sitting in front of a blank sheet waiting for inspiration – get something down. Write against the clock in bursts of about fifteen minutes, and then pause to review and reflect, and eventually to polish. Also, you must always have some audience in mind; even diaries seem to address some imaginary reader. Tell your story TO someone and write, not just to please yourself, but to reach this imagined audience. The other bit of good advice I would offer you is learn to write as accurately and grammatically as you can. Artists have to learn to draw before they can take liberties – you can't break the rules till you know what they are! Learning the craft of writing well gives you greater choice and freedom in the end.

In small groups, discuss what Jan Mark has to say about writing:

1 What age group does she prefer to write for? Why?
2 Why does she like to write books with a science fiction or historical background?
3 Why does she think that children's books should also be interesting for adults?
4 What two pieces of advice about writing are contained in the last paragraph of the interview?

Decide the age group

First of all, decide what age group you are going to aim at – any age between *seven* and *twelve*. Skills of reading, understanding and maturity will vary a great deal from child to child, so you'll need to be flexible, but it's a good idea to visualise a particular audience for your writing – age, sex, interests, reading skills, etc – as it makes it so much easier to find the appropriate language for your story.

Find the right books

Now find out what kind of books are popular with that age group, by asking questions of anyone who might know – children themselves, parents, the local children's librarian, primary school teachers, etc. Some things will have universal appeal: humour, fantasy, and a certain element of the frightening (but not too much). A recent survey of eight to nine year olds found Roald Dahl top favourite, with books like *Charlie and the Chocolate Factory; The Witches; George's Marvellous Medicine* coming near the top of most children's lists. Do you remember reading some of these yourself? If so, you could jot down what you think were the ingredients which appealed to you at that age.

Read the story and review it

Read one of the stories recommended to you. You might like to read one of the stories by Jan Mark mentioned in the interview. You could choose a short one so it won't take you too long.

↝ Now write a review of the story for parents who might think of buying it for their children for Christmas. Tell them the factual things like the author, title and price (publisher and ISBN number would be useful, too) and your considered opinion of it for that age group. You could also say what kind of children it would most appeal to. Are there illustrations? If so, what do you think of them, and, if not, do you feel the lack of them?

Don't be afraid to make criticisms; you are not writing a publishers' 'blurb' to sell the book but appraising it. Imagine you are a critic on a

newspaper, preparing a short item for the 'Christmas Books for Children' page.

Make a display of your reviews so all the class can share them.

And then he would have to tell Ezzie all about it, every detail, how one recess long ago the boys had decided to put some girls in the school trash cans. It had been one of those suggestions that stuns everyone with its rightness. Someone had said, 'Hey, let's put those girls over there in the trash cans!' and the plan won immediate acceptance. Nothing could have been more appropriate. The trash cans were big and had just been emptied, and in an instant the boys were off chasing the girls and yelling at the tops of their lungs.

It had been wonderful at first, Mouse remembered. Primitive blood had raced through his body. The desire to capture had driven him like a wild man through the school yard, up the sidewalk, everywhere. He understood what had driven the cave man and the barbarian, because this same passion was driving him. Putting the girls in the trash cans was the most important challenge of his life. His long screaming charge ended with him red-faced, gasping for breath – and with Viola Angotti pinned against the garbage cans.

His moment of triumph was short. It lasted about two seconds. Then it began to dim as he realized, first, that it *was* Viola Angotti, and, second, that he was not going to be able to get her into the garbage can without a great deal of help.

He cried, 'Hey, you guys, come on, I've got one,' but behind him the school yard was silent. Where was everybody? he had wondered uneasily. As it turned out, the principal had caught the other boys, and they were all being marched back in the front door of the school, but Mouse didn't know this.

He called again, 'Come on, you guys, get the lid off this garbage can, will you?'

And then, when he said that, Viola Angotti had taken two steps forward. She said, 'Nobody's putting *me* in no garbage can.' He could still remember how she had looked standing there. She had recently taken the part of the Statue of Liberty in a class play, and somehow she seemed taller and stronger at this moment than when she had been in costume.

He cried, 'Hey, you guys!' It was a plea. 'Where are you?'

And then Viola Angotti had taken one more step, and with a faint sigh she had socked him in the stomach so hard that he had doubled over and lost his lunch. He hadn't known it was possible to be hit like that outside a boxing ring. It was the hardest blow he had ever taken. Viola Angotti could be heavyweight champion of the world.

As she walked past his crumpled body she had said again, 'Nobody's putting me in no garbage can.' It had sounded like one of the world's basic truths. The sun will rise. The tides will flow. Nobody's putting Viola Angotti in no garbage can.

Later, when he thought about it, he realized that he had been lucky. If she had wanted to, Viola Angotti could have capped her victory by tossing his rag-doll body into the garbage can and slamming down the lid. Then, when the principal came out on to the playground calling, 'Benjamin Fawley! Has anybody seen Benjamin Fawley?' he would have had to moan. 'I'm in here.' He would have had to climb out of the garbage can in front of the whole school. His shame would have followed him for life. When he was a grown man, people would still be pointing him out to their children. '*That*'s the man that Viola Angotti stuffed into the garbage can.'

After you have read it, discuss the following questions with a partner. They should give you some ideas of how to construct your own story:

- What would you say is the climax of the incident?
- How does it build up to this?
- How do we find out about the characters involved?
- Where does the humour come in?

Your own story for children

You are now ready to try your hand at writing your own story, or at least part of one.

Stage 1

Make some decisions about your story: funny? fantasy? central character? setting?

Stage 2

Next make a plan for the story, stage by stage:

1 Description of where it takes place.
2 Introduction of central character(s).
3 Some event or incident occurs.
4 What happens as a result?

It doesn't matter if you can't find a conclusion for your story; you could break it off quite suddenly if you like and leave it to the readers to predict what might happen next.

Stage 3

When you have a rough draft of the story, read it through to a friend; suggestions and criticisms at this stage can help a lot and, if you get stuck, sometimes a fresh mind can see how to move it on.

Stage 4

Now revise and correct your draft, proofreading for spelling and grammar at the same time, and produce your final version.

LOOK BACK

You'll want to put this into your folder, but perhaps you could also read it aloud to a suitable audience – a group of Year 7 pupils in your own school or a primary school class of the appropriate age group. If yours is one of those which leaves the children to complete the story, the teacher might let you read what they conclude later. This could be a very interesting way of assessing the success of your story.

You could record the reactions of your audience at the end of the copy you put into your folder. Make sure, too, you give it a heading which explains exactly what you were doing and for whom it was intended.

5

POETRY
FOR CHILDREN

Can you remember any of the games and
rhymes you used to chant in the playground
when you first started school? What about the
first poems that you read? In this section you
will be looking at the kinds of rhymes and
poems that appeal to children.

Traditional rhymes

Many rhymes and traditional games are handed
down from generation to generation with a few
changes in the words to bring them up to date.
Some rhymes have regional variations, too, and
many parts of the country have traditional
rhymes of their own.

This one is a clapping game, with an elaborate
ritual of movements.

> Under the bramble bushes,
> Down by the sea.
> Boom, boom boom.
> True love for you, my darling,
> True love for me.
> And when we are married,
> We'll raise a family,
> A boy for you and a girl for me.
> And that's the way that it shall be.
> Under the bramble bushes...

Many of these rhymes have a circular nature, as
this one does.

Here's a skipping rhyme. Do you know one like it?

Sea shells, cockle shells,
Eevy ivy over.
How many boys did you kiss last night?
One? two? three?...

Research into rhymes

✒ For this project divide into groups of three or four.

1 See how many kinds of rhyme you can remember between you; get one of the group to write them down.

2 Now take your research outside school. Those of you who have young brothers and sisters could ask them, and you could all ask parents, grandparents, members of staff or other adults what rhymes they remember from their childhoods. If the rhymes go with a special game, ask them to explain that briefly. Make notes of all you find out and bring your material back to the group discussion in another lesson. There may be a book in your school library that will tell you about traditional playground games: there is a famous one called *The Language and Lore of Schoolchildren* by Iona and Peter Opie.

3 Share out all the examples you have between you so that each person can make one sheet of a communal booklet. Write out the chosen rhymes, with simple instructions where appropriate, and illustrate them if you can.

What kind of poetry appeals to young children?

⟿ In groups of three or four, discuss what you think young children enjoy in poetry.

Rhyme is important

You'll probably agree that rhyme is important. You may remember even now some of the rhymes you were read when you were very young – and how quickly you learned to repeat them. It's well known that rhyme is a considerable aid to memory, and perhaps it appeals to something very primitive in all of us.

What other ingredients, besides rhyme, do young children like in verse? Between you, see if you can remember a couple of nursery rhymes all the way through, and think just what they contain.

A serious element

Tom, Tom, the Piper's son
Stole a pig and away did run
The pig was eat
And Tom was beat
And he ran howling down the street.

This is not entirely a jolly rhyme, is it? It's about a theft and there's an element of violence in it, too, but it certainly isn't about serious crime or child abuse. It could be that the bits of 'real life' in children's rhymes are made easier to cope with because of the rhyme, the rhythm and the humour.

The Ring O' Roses game so popular with very young children actually refers to the plague of the 1660s: the first symptom was often a sneeze ('Tishoo!') and the disease was distinguished by the circles of red which appeared on the skin. You can guess what 'All fall down!' meant! It may be that we can all cope with things more easily if we can joke about them. What about the examples you remembered? Do any of them have any serious content?

Children like the ridiculous

Children like poems where logic has been completely abandoned or the world turned upside down:

A careless old man from Blackheath,
Sat down on his set of false teeth.
He said, in his pain,
'Ive done it again,
I have bitten myself underneath.'

Your own poems for children

⟿ Keeping in mind what you have learned about the kinds of poetry that appeals to children, you are now going to write your own poems for young children. At the end of this project you will have a small anthology of poems. If you like, you could write your poems with a particular young child in mind (say a younger brother or sister).

The easiest way to set about writing your poems is to use other poems as your models. It's not much use sitting and waiting for inspiration – get going by imitating poems that you think will appeal to young children.

1 Why not start with a *limerick*? You have probably written limericks before. If not, the following might inspire you:

There was a Young Lady whose chin
Resembled the point of a pin:
So she had it made sharp,
And purchased a harp,
And played several tunes with her chin.

Edward Lear

A wonderful bird is the pelican,
His mouth can hold more than his belican,
He can take in his beak
Enough food for a week –
I'm dammed if I know how the helican.

Anon

2 You could include an *acrostic poem* – with a secret message hidden in it, like this one:

TRUE LOVE

Glenys,
Every moment
That I am away from you seems
Like an eternity
Only the heavy demands of business
Separate me from my one
True love.

If your anthology is for a particular child, you could use his/her name for the acrostic.

3 Here are a couple of Spike Milligan poems which depend on a last line of anti-climax:

Mary Pugh
Was nearly two
When she went out of doors.
She went out standing up she did
But came back on all fours.
The moral of the story
Please meditate and pause:
Never send a baby out
With loosely waisted draws.

You could start:

Tommy Moore
Was nearly four...

You must never bath in an Irish Stew
It's a most illogical thing to do
But should you persist against my reasoning
Don't fail to add the appropriate seasoning.

You could start:

Never wash in a bucket of glue...

Remember that the rhymes will be an important ingredient in its success with very young children, so pay special attention to getting these and the bouncy rhythms right.

4 How about a *nonsense poem*?
There are lots of traditional ones which have lasted a very long time.

I eat my peas with honey.
I've done so all my life.
It makes the peas taste funny,
But it keeps them on the knife!

Try:

I take my fish with mustard.
I've done so all my life . . . . .

Here's another traditional one:

The Man in the Wilderness asked of me
'How many blackberries grow in the sea?'
I answered him as I thought good,
'As many red herrings as grow in the wood.'

The Man in the Wilderness asked me why
His hen could swim, and his pig could fly.
I answered him briskly as I thought best,
'Because they were born in a cuckoo's nest.'

The man in the Wilderness asked me to tell
The sands in the sea and I counted them well.
Says he with a grin, 'And not one more?'
I answered him bravely, 'You go and make sure!'

ANON

Try your own version of this, too. Keep the first line, but make up your own questions for the Man in the Wilderness to ask – as crazy as you like – and your own answers.

If you want some more models for nonsense poetry, look in the school library for those of Lewis Carroll and Edward Lear; they will give you some more ideas.

5 If you want to include a serious poem, what about this traditional American Indian curse (page 29) as a model?

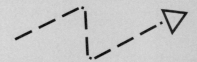

6 Another idea is *puzzle poems* and *riddles*. You could find some of these in children's books or comics, to show you what to aim for.

Putting the anthology together

You should now have enough material to make your anthology of poems for children. Your anthology could include:

1 the rhymes you collected at the beginning of this section;
2 any poems you liked when you were finding poems to imitate;
3 your own poems.

You could illustrate some of the poems to add interest. When you have finished, staple the pages of your anthology together and create a cover for it.

LOOK BACK

If your anthology was created with a particular child in mind, what was his or her reaction to it?
You could present your anthology to a local playgroup or school, but make sure you have made copies for your coursework folder first. If there are comments on the material, include this in your coursework folder.

A SPELL TO DESTROY LIFE

Listen!
   Now I have come to step over your soul
      (I know your clan)
      (I know your name)
      (I have stolen your spit and buried it under earth)
   I bury your soul under earth
   I cover you over with black rock
   I cover you over with black cloth
   I cover you over with black slabs
   You disappear forever

   Your path leads to the
                  Black Coffin
                     in the hills of the Darkening Land

   So let it be for you

   The clay of the hills covers you
   The black clay of the Darkening Land

   Your soul fades away

   It becomes blue (colour of despair)
   When darkness comes your spirit shrivels and
                  dwindles to disappear forever
Listen!

Cherokee Indians (NORTH AMERICA)

29

6

INFORMATION FOR CHILDREN

—

In this section you will be deciding what children need to know and how this differs from information for adults in content, style and presentation. This will involve you in research, selection, adaptation and revision. You will be producing a collection of pieces to demonstrate your ability to write information texts for a particular audience for a particular purpose.

A guide to your own school

⚡ Look at the poem by Roger McGough on page 31, and discuss it with a partner:

1 What age is the child in the poem?
2 What stage has he/she reached in his/her schooling?
3 What misunderstandings does the child make?
4 Would any of the child's fears and confusions also apply to a newcomer to secondary school?

First Day at School

A millionbillionwillion miles from home
Waiting for the bell to go. (To go where?)
Why are they all so big, other children?
So noisy? So much at home they
must have been born in uniform
Lived all their lives in playgrounds
Spent the years inventing games
that don't let me in. Games
that are rough, that swallow you up.

And the railings.
All around, the railings.
Are they to keep out wolves and monsters?
Things that carry off and eat children?
Things you don't take sweets from?
Perhaps they're to stop us getting out
Running away from the lessins. Lessin.
What does a lessin look like?
Sounds small and slimy.
They keep them in glassrooms.
Whole rooms made out of glass. Imagine.

I wish I could remember my name
Mummy said it would come in useful.
Like wellies. When there's puddles.
Yellowwellies. I wish she was here.
I think my name is sewn on somewhere
Perhaps the teacher will read it for me.
Tea-cher. The one who makes the tea.

Memories of the first week at school

Do you remember what it felt like to be a newcomer in your present school? You had probably visited it before and met some of the staff responsible for your year, but when you actually arrived on that first morning, it felt quite different, didn't it?

Working in pairs, jot down some of the memories you have of the first week. Did you get lost? Did you forget your books or lose your bag? Maybe you were given a map of the school, or some sort of guide book? If so, did this tell you what you really needed to know? What information would you *like* to have been given? Make a list between you.

Here is an extract from a prospectus for a community comprehensive school; it is clearly aimed at parents who are considering choosing the school for their child.

The school opened in September 1978 as a Community School which not only caters for 11–16 pupils as a comprehensive school but also meets the needs of anyone who wishes to learn throughout their life. It is very much a family school where families can learn together. It has special provision for Art and Design, Technology, Home Economics, Drama, Music and Computer Studies as part of its community role and it organises a wide range of day and evening class activities for adults and young people.

1. Learning is a life-long process and not something you can cram in between the ages of 5 and 16.

2. The task of a school is to provide equal opportunities for children whatever their abilities.

3. Children are not equal; they are different and unique and should be allowed to develop accordingly.

4. As far as resources allow, learning should be individualised to meet the needs of each child as they emerge and develop.

5. The school curriculum should be as broad as possible for as long as possible.

6. A curriculum is only relevant when it is in close contact with the community – parents, industry and commerce and is outward and forward looking.

7. It is the whole curriculum which gives purpose to learning and not a "hotch potch" of individual subjects.

8. Children only learn effectively when teachers and parents co-operate to provide support and encouragement.

↗ Still in the same pairs, discuss which bits of information would be equally useful to a new student. Which parts would have little interest for him/her? Would an eleven year old understand all the language here?

An alternative guide to school

↗You are going to produce an Alternative Guide for New Students – for your own school.

In your pairs discuss what the contents of this guide should be, and then share the writing of it between you. Think about including the following:

1 sketch map showing the location of certain vital places (what would a new student want to know?);
2 some information about teachers. It's best to avoid individual profiles (for obvious reasons!) but you could compose lists of things that annoy teachers most, and ways of keeping on the right side of teachers;
3 some frank and unofficial views on school food might be useful;
4 music and drama activities;
5 clubs and societies;
6 the school library (the range of books and when it is open);
7 any drawings or cartoons that would liven up the guide.

When you've made your list of all the sections, divide these between you and start writing. (Your own individual contribution will have to be clearly indicated in your GCSE folder.) Stop from time to time to consult your partner and try out on him/her bits that you've written.

When it's all finished and stapled together as a booklet, perhaps your librarian would display the final products in the library for those who have been in the school for only a short time to comment on. Feedback from your intended audience will be valuable for your future writing.

Write a poem about school

Look back at the poem by Roger McGough. Compare the experience of the child in the poem with your own memories of your first week at secondary school.

↗ Now see if you can write your own poem (which can be quite short, if you like) about the feelings of a Year 7 pupil arriving at your present school, using McGough's as a model. But base the poem on your own memories.

1 What fears and misunderstanding are there likely to be?
2 What feelings will you record?
3 Make the language appropriate to the child speaking.

You will need to make a first draft and then revise it at least once, rearranging lines, replacing words and correcting spelling.

A guide book to your own area

Here is an extract from an imaginary Town Guide.

One of the most pleasant of Barfordshire's market towns, Oldford is the economic and commercial centre of the West Barfordshire District. It is situated between Barford and the Gloucestershire border, is served by the A27 main road and is within easy reach of the M8 and M13 motorways. It is, too, on the banks of the lovely Rushing river and is set between that river's tranquil lowlands and the broad sweep of the Cotswold Hills.

For centuries Oldford has been linked with the making of woollen cloth and its famous blankets. There has, in recent times, been a decline in the blanket industry but the town continues to flourish with the introduction of modern technological industries that are largely based on the small industrial estates on the town's outskirts. The town's population is at present 17,500 but it is expected to rise to 21,000 by 1996.

To cope with its present and projected residential development, Oldford has several modern and well planned housing estates. The new East Oldford development offers accommodation to suit most people's requirements, including those of young families and retired people.

The town has an excellent shopping centre and in the tree lined streets of the old town there are many individual and specialist shops. Market days see these shops and streets thronged with people.

As a tourist centre Oldford has a great deal to offer. Its many old and interesting buildings are set in a beautiful countryside with the old town of Little Vale and the charming Cotswold villages not far away. These are ample facilities for leisure including the excellent Rushing Sports Centre. The town, too, has a wide range of both state and independent schools. It has, in short, all the amenities of a modern town yet in the traditional setting of a country town that has enjoyed a long history.

It is clear that the guide is aimed at adults, but how exactly do we know that?

➤ Work with a partner and find evidence to prove it:

1 *in the content*
What kinds of things does it tell us?
What features of the town are stressed?
2 *in the language*
Are the sentences complicated?
Are there any difficult words?

Between you, jot down as many points as you can, for a class discussion.

If you were aiming at a younger age group, what aspects of the town would be interesting and/or attractive? What kind of things would young people of your age or less want to know about a place if their family were considering a move there, or even a holiday? With your partner, make a list of all the amenities *they* might be looking for (swimming pool, Sports Centre, bus services, etc.)

➤ On your own, prepare a section of a Guide to Your Own Area (village, small town, district of a larger town) aimed at young people of your own age and less. Your could include a sketch map and illustrations if you like, and remember that all young people reading it may not have the same interests as you, so cater for their needs, too, in your guide.

The information doesn't need to be all complimentary; if you think the facilities for young people in your area are poor, then say so, and suggest what could be done to improve them.

LOOK BACK

Make a display of the work, so that everyone can share what you have written, and after you have seen the rest, write a short paragraph assessing the success of your own guide (which can be included in your coursework folder).

Writing for information

Volcanoes

Though a volcano is commonly thought of as a somewhat conical landform, the upper part of which has a funnel-shaped depression called a crater, the image is valid only for some volcanoes. Fissure volcanoes, for example, occur along fractures or series of fractures that may be several kilometres in length, where molten-rock material within the Earth, magma, is ejected from the fractures and forms great layers of volcanic rock at the surface. A volcano is best-defined as any region of the Earth in which magma has erupted one or more times through the ages. No part of the Earth was free of volcanic eruptions during geological time, but in historic time, volcanic activity has been limited to well-defined regions.

About 62 percent of the world's active volcanoes occur along the margins of the Pacific Ocean; 45 percent are located in the arcuate land chains or island arcs of the eastern Pacific, and 17 percent occur along principal mountain belts in the western parts of North and South America. There are strikingly large areas without any active volcanoes in the regions between Alaska and the Cascade Mountains of the western United States and in northern Chile; but many extinct volcanoes exist in both areas. Another 14 percent of the world's active volcanoes are distributed over the Indonesian island arc. Approximately 17 percent, combined, occur on the central Pacific islands (3 percent), on the islands of the Indian Ocean (1 percent), and on the Atlantic islands (13 percent). The remaining 7 percent is accounted for by occurrences in the Mediterranean and northern Asia Minor regions and in the centres of the continents, especially upon the East African Rift Valley system.

Volcanic eruptions in inhabited areas have been the causes of disastrous loss of life and property. Data collected from the year 1500 to 1914 suggest that volcanic eruptions may have caused the loss of about 190,000 human lives. It should be noted, however, that associated sea waves, mud slides, and other catastrophic events that accompany eruptions often cause additional fatalities.

This is a section from the entry on volcanoes in the *Encyclopaedia Britannica* – the best known standard work of reference. There's probably a copy of it, in numerous volumes, in your school library, and you will certainly find one in the public library. This entry is very informative but it might not seem very attractive to a casual reader, especially a young one. It is intended, of course, for someone who is looking very specifically for this information and not just browsing.

Writing a fact sheet

🖎 What difficulties would an eight to ten year old encounter here? Working with a partner, make a list of these: note words that might not be understood (if there are any that are unfamiliar to *you*, look them up in a dictionary); and any other features that might make it a difficult text, like length of sentences or use of statistics.

Now see what could be done with the information to make it more attractive to the younger age group, though still informative and accurate. Select from the facts what you think is appropriate and decide if pictures and diagrams would help to make it more easily understood. When the two of you have come to agreement on these points, produce between you a Fact Sheet on Volcanoes for use in a primary school.

You'll need further information from suitable reference books in the library, or the rest of the long entry in the *Encyclopaedia Britannica*. Keep in mind the children you are writing for: add illustrations and headlines to break up the text – and be selective! Don't swamp them with too much information.

Share the sections between you, and indicate on the finished product who wrote what, for your GCSE folder.

Trying it out

You could make a display for the Library or offer your sheets to a Geography or Science teacher for a Year 7 class. This way you will get a consumer's reaction, although it will be from a slightly older age band.

Writing on a topic that interests you

You have now thought carefully about presenting information in an attractive and interesting way. You can also apply what you have learnt to a subject of your own choice.

🖎 Select a topic which interests you and which you know at least a little about to begin with; the subject could be drawn from Natural History, like 'Dinosaurs' or 'Garden Birds'; or a leisure activity, like 'Cycling' or 'Computer Games'. Some area of History which interests you would be a good idea, or a geographical topic.

Use the resources of your school library, plus any specialised information you may have at home. Remember, if you are using an encyclopaedia, use the Index Volume so you don't miss any relevant sections.

The information can be presented either as an article for a magazine aimed at eight to ten year olds or another fact sheet like the one you did on volcanoes. If you choose to do an article it may give more scope for personal comments – saying what appeals to you about the subject and how you first became interested; the fact sheet needs to be rather more impersonal in style, but still entertaining. If you can't draw your own illustrations, you could photocopy them from a reference book.

LOOK BACK

As with the volcanoes sheet, try to find a suitable audience for your work, and see how it fulfils its purpose.

7

MOUNTING A CAMPAIGN

—

You have already learned a lot about presenting information for a younger audience. In this section you will be looking at information extracts with a 'message'.

Public service leaflets

The following extracts are all from 'public service' leaflets. That is, they all have a 'message' for the reader which could generally be agreed as being helpful to society.

First read them carefully to yourself, thinking about the intended audience – adults or children? what age group?

BUSCODE

IT'S COOL TO KNOW HOW TO SURVIVE - IT'S DUMB TO BECOME A TRAFFIC ACCIDENT STATISTIC.

FOLLOW THE CODE KEEP DEATH OFF THE ROAD BE SMART **THINK FIRST!**

THINK FIRST

FIND A SAFE PLACE TO CROSS THEN STOP

USE YOUR EYES & EARS LOOK ALL ROUND FOR TRAFFIC AND LISTEN

GETTING TO THE BUS

THE YOUNG PERSONS CODE FOR SAFE TRAVEL BY BUS OR COACH

WAIT TILL IT'S SAFE

IF TRAFFIC IS COMING - LET IT PASS - LOOK ALL ROUND AGAIN

LOOK AND LISTEN AGAIN WHEN THERE'S NO TRAFFIC NEAR .... WALK STRAIGHT ACROSS THE ROAD

ARRIVE ALIVE KEEP LOOKING AND LISTENING FOR TRAFFIC WHEN YOU CROSS

ROUNDABOUTS

110 When approaching a roundabout, watch out for traffic already on it. Take special care to look out for cyclists or motorcyclists ahead or to the side. Give way to traffic on your right unless road markings indicate otherwise; but keep moving if the way is clear. At some junctions there may be more than one roundabout. At each, apply the normal rules for roundabouts. Keep a special look out for the 'Give Way' lines.

111 Where there are two lanes at the entrance to a round-about, unless signs or road markings indicate otherwise:
When turning left:
Approach in the left-hand lane; keep to that lane in the round-about.
When going forward:
Approach in the left-hand lane; keep to that lane in the round-about. If conditions dictate (for example, if the left-hand lane is blocked), approach in the right-hand lane; keep to that lane in the roundabout. If the roundabout itself is clear of other traffic, take the most convenient lane through the roundabout.
When turning right:
Approach in the right-hand lane; keep to that lane in the round-about.

112 When there are more than two lanes at the entrance to a roundabout, unless signs or road markings indicate otherwise, use the clearest convenient lane on approach and through the round-about suitable for the exit you intend to take.

113 When in a roundabout, look out for and show consideration to other vehicles crossing in front of you, especially those intending to leave by the next exit. Show particular consideration for cyclists and motorcyclists.

from *The Highway Code*

Toothbrushing with care

Most of us brush our teeth. But very few of us brush them well enough. Help your children learn to brush their teeth really well at least once every day. Make it a part of your family's everyday routine.

WHAT YOU CAN DO

■ Start brushing your child's teeth at an early age. Then it's a habit right from the start.

■ Help with tooth-brushing, at least until your child is eight years old. When your child takes over brushing, check that it's done well enough. Every surface of every tooth should be well brushed – both sides as well as the chewing surface, and the back teeth as well as the front, both top and bottom. Use a toothbrush with a small head and a pea-sized blob of fluoride toothpaste.

"David does his own teeth now but I like to help Thomas to make sure the back ones are done properly."

THE NEW ENVIRONMENTAL POLICY

Governments across the world are re-appraising their attitudes to the environment. Environmental plans encompassing everything from domestic waste, to contributions to conventions on global environmental issues are being prepared, new measures are being considered, costs and benefits are being calculated. The Netherlands has a new National Environmental Policy Plan; France is discussing a 'Plan Vert'; Sweden has introduced environmental taxes as part of a tax reform system; Norway plans green taxes for 1991; Denmark plans an expansion of its existing environmental tax system; and Britain has produced an extensive White Paper on environment policy.

from a leaflet published by British Gas

Analyse the leaflets

➢ Work in small groups of three or four and discuss your impressions of these examples. Between you, decide what age group each is aimed at. Then ask yourselves *how* you decided this. For each example, make a list of your reasons under these headings:

Subject matter: What was there in the things said that gave you clues?
Language: Make a note of difficult vocabulary and long complex sentences.
Pictures: Whom would they attract and how? (colour? humour?) How did the illustrations add to the message?

Check your conclusions in discussion with the rest of the class.

Your own campaign – healthier eating

Work in the same small groups and decide how you will mount a Campaign for Healthier Eating – this time aimed at nine to ten year olds. Most of the information you will need is contained in the leaflet below, which was written to appeal to young adults. You could add to this any further material you find from library books, or leaflets from your school's Home Economics Department.

First of all you'll have to decide what differences in content, language and presentation you will make to appeal to a younger group. Decisions as to what you'll put in and what leave out should be made as a group, but then you can share out the tasks between you.

You should aim to produce:

1 a short informative leaflet;
2 one or two posters to be put up in primary schools;
3 a 'public service' commercial for TV;
4 an article for a page in a newspaper aimed at youngsters of this age.

YOUR GUIDE TO SENSIBLE EATING

This is the time of life when increasingly you can make your own decisions about shopping for food and preparing meals as well as deciding what to eat when you're away from home. A good diet with the right balance of nutrients, coupled with regular exercise, is all part of a modern healthy lifestyle. But now it's up to you.

This brief guide will help you choose a balanced diet to provide your body with everything it needs for the way you live today. It also contains some advice on areas that often cause concern.

EAT A VARIETY OF FOODS

The basis of a balanced diet is choosing a variety of foods from the four main groups — cereals (bread, rice, oats, pasta and breakfast cereals); meat and alternatives (eggs, fish, beans and nuts); dairy foods (cheese, milk and yogurt); and fruits and vegetables. Fats and oils (butter, margarine and cooking oils) should be used in smaller quantities.

For a good balance, eat more from the cereal and fruit and vegetable groups. Go easy on the fats, oils and fatty foods which can provide more calories than you need and as eating too much

fat may also increase the chance of heart problems in later life. Go for lean meat, poultry or fish, and choose spreads which are high in polyunsaturates. Try to avoid eating chips too often — a baked potato makes a good change.

Watch your salt intake too. We tend to eat more salt than we need and an excess may, in susceptible individuals, contribute to high blood pressure, which is itself a risk factor in many other illnesses.

Eat more bread and cereals (preferably wholegrain) as well as a variety of fruit, vegetables and pulses (beans etc): this will give you a good intake of dietary fibre which helps with the speedy and easy elimination of waste from the body, keeps your digestive system healthy, and helps prevent constipation.

HEALTHY ADVICE

- Some teenagers are plagued by spots which often seem to appear at the most inconvenient times. It

is a popular belief that chocolate, fatty foods and soft drinks can all aggravate acne. Although there is no good evidence to substantiate this, for some individuals cutting down on confectionery or fatty foods does seem to help. Eating wholemeal bread, polyunsaturated margarine and plenty of vegetables may also help.

- Frequent intakes of sugary foods such as sweets, biscuits, puddings and soft drinks — especially between meals — can damage teeth. Taken occasionally, particularly after a meal, sweet foods do no harm but it is a good idea to brush your teeth afterwards. Remember to change your toothbrush when it shows signs of wear and keep a six monthly date with your dentist.

- Sudden 'spurts of growth' may start at about 11 years if you're a girl and a little later, at around 13 or 14 years, in boys. At this time, a big appetite may well mean you'll need to eat more than your parents but choose nutritious foods rather than snacks high in sugar or fat.

- Fast take-away foods can be nutritious but it makes sense to avoid too many fatty foods and ring the changes. Instead of burger and chips you could try a baked potato, a pizza, chicken tandoori or chicken chow mein.

- Being overweight can spoil good looks and make you more susceptible to a number of health problems in later life. If you're carrying surplus pounds,

aim to hold your weight constant so that you will gradually slim down as you continue to grow. Watch your sugar and fat intake and avoid too many cakes, biscuits and sweets. It's a good idea to take more exercise too. But, whatever you do, beware of extreme, excessive slimming.

KEEPING FIT

Regular exercise helps keep your body in shape. When muscles are used regularly, they

stay firm and you look good. So try to include exercise as part of your day.

Walk or cycle to work or school instead of catching a bus. Two or three times a week take some more strenuous exercise as part of your leisure activities. Football, cycling, dancing, ice-skating, tennis, aerobics and swimming are all good exercise. Keep up team games if you enjoy them and check out what your local sports or leisure centre has to offer. Now might be a good time to try something new — like sailboarding, riding or basketball.

LOOK BACK

Share your work with others in the group; make a display, or try out your posters and leaflets on the younger pupils in your school. Perhaps posters could go up in the school dining room?

Put a copy of your work in your GCSE folder, or the whole group's work if you like, with your contribution clearly labelled. Ask yourself if you really got over the message of *Healthy and Enjoyable Eating*.

8

HAVE YOU GOT IT RIGHT?

—

You have already looked at material by the experts, the people who earn a living writing for children. You have also tried out your own work on a younger audience. In this section you will be looking at two other ways to test your material: seeing how adverts work and testing for readability.

Advertisements

Advertisers have to be aware of their audience – they earn their living by selling products and ideas to people. If they get it wrong, they are out of a job!

Look at the two very different advertisements on page 42 aimed to attract the attention of young people.

⚡▷ The RSPCA advert is not trying to sell anything. It is trying to put over a message (an idea). With a partner, discuss what means it is using to do this. Discuss its appeal and how successful you think it is in doing what it sets out to do. Think about:

1 the impact of the photographs;
2 the language that is used;
3 how the advert is set out on the page.

⚡▷ The Wella advert is trying to sell you something. The advertisers want you to go out and buy the product. How does this one work? With your partner, consider the following:

1 the brand name;
2 use of puns;
3 contribution of the photograph;
4 short sentences and snappy phrases;
5 anything else that contributes to its effect.

How successful is it?

Next, discuss what ages of young people each of these two advertisements is geared to. Where do you think they may have appeared? Can you think of any others you have seen recently that are similar?

Making an advert

Stage 1 – research

Neither of these makes use of one of the most effective weapons of the advertiser – humour. See what examples you can find for yourselves of adverts which are aimed at young people or children, and which make use of humour.

The most productive area for your research is likely to be TV. Note down any good examples while you are watching and bring your notes to a class discussion. Or you can look through magazines, comics, etc and see if you can find some examples there.

Stage 2 – choose an advert you like

Choose any one advertisement you like, either on TV or in print, and analyse its appeal. If it is a TV one, describe briefly what it contains; if it's a printed one, you could cut it out and stick it into your work. Consider the age group, and the type of person it is intended for, where (or when) it appears, what means it uses to attract attention, the kind of language, the visual appeal and anything else that adds to it.

Stage 3 – invent the product and plan how to market it

Work in groups of three or four for this. You are going to invent a new product and plan how to market it.

1 Decide first what the product will be: you could invent a new healthy 'product' to tie in with your work in the last section.
2 What age group are you aiming at?
3 Do you want children to buy your product or will parents be buying it for children?
4 Are there any other gimmicks, like money-off coupons or special gifts with tokens, that might help your campaign?
5 The *brand* name will be an important collective decision: success may easily depend on it and it must sound distinctive and different from its competitors.

Stage 4 – the printed advert

When you have made these joint decisions, each one individually should sketch out an idea for a printed advertisement to appear in some magazine or newspaper. Bring these back to another meeting of the team and compare ideas, make suggestions for improvements and perhaps find some snappy catch phrases that all the adverts will include.

You can now make a fair copy of your idea for your folder, with notes about the joint decisions you made earlier.

Stage 5 – make a commercial

Back in your groups, invent a commercial for TV for your product. Discuss it first, decide on content, general lines of the dialogue, which of you is to play which role, and rehearse it as an improvisation, to be presented to the rest of the class when you are satisfied

LOOK BACK

Which of the commercials did you think worked best? What were the ingredients that succeeded? Which products would be easiest to sell?

The second method of testing your work is one which has been designed by educational experts. This is called 'readability'.

There have been many attempts to devise scientific ways of testing the reading difficulties of texts. Some of the these systems are very complicated but the technique explained below is a relatively simple one. You can use this method to test the 'readability level' of some of the language you have been considering in this book.

Testing for readability

There is no need to sample many passages for the purposes of this exercise. Working with a partner:

1 Choose one of the pieces from the 'Voices from the Past' section (pages 11–13) and test it according to the instructions.

2 Choose any extract from the 'Information for Children' section (pages 30–35) and check on its readability level – perhaps the *Britannica* entry on volcanoes, or the town guide?

3 Now test some of your own pieces: at least one from each of you. Did the age group you were aiming at coincide with the reading level?

If it didn't, don't worry too much. There is an important factor left out of all these calculations – the motivation of the reader. If the subject matter is interesting enough, difficult vocabulary and complex sentences prove much less of a problem. Also, if the difficult bits are explained in the course of the piece of writing, that lessens the problems, too. So, although it is interesting to test your work in this way, and in some cases it may make you aware of difficulties you need to take into consideration, the attractiveness and the interest of the writing far outweigh the readability in importance.

A safer and more important test is to try out what you have written on sample audiences of the right age group, as you have been doing throughout this book.

---

1) Select a number of samples from a text whose difficulty you wish to estimate. Each sample should contain one hundred words. You might, for example, take the first one hundred words from every tenth page, starting with the first complete sentence.

2) Count the total number of *complete* sentences in your sample. Count the number of words in these complete sentences. Then calculate the average sentence length by dividing the number of words by the number of sentences.

3) Count the number of words of three of more syllables in the total sample. Divide this number by the number of one hundred word samples. This gives the percentage of long words in the sample.

4) Obtain the Fog Index by adding
   (a) the average sentence length, and
   (b) percentage of long words.
Then multiply this total by 0.4. This figure represents the grade level for which the material is appropriate in terms of difficulty. Equivalent ages for grade levels:

   Grade 1–6 years
   Grade 2–7 years
   Grade 3–8 years etc.

Source: Open University Reading Development Course

9

FINAL PROJECT –
A MAGAZINE FOR
YOUNG PEOPLE

—

You have now learnt a lot about adapting language, content and presentation to the audience you are aiming for; at the same time, you have become more aware of the wide range of styles of English which exist for different purposes.

You can put this knowledge to good use by completing this unit of work with a project – to produce a magazine for young people (*you* choose the age group – anything between eight and thirteen), which they will find attractive and entertaining as well as informative.

Research – what is available

Look, before you start, at some of the pages, or separate magazines, produced by certain newspapers for young people. The *Guardian* has a *Young Guardian* page, the *Daily Telegraph* produces a special supplement on Saturdays, while *The Times* and the *Independent* bring out separate issues, called *Early Times* and *The Indy*. Some of these are sure to be in your school library, and perhaps your teacher can get hold of others for you, if there aren't people in your class who subscribe to them.

Here are a few extracts, to illustrate the range of subject matter you'll find in them. Some articles are clearly written by young people themselves; others are by adults to inform and appeal to the readers.

Getting started

First you will need to decide on the general age group you are appealing to; there's no need to be too specific as interests and reading skills vary so much.

You can choose to take any special line you like; concentrate on current affairs, if you want, or look for subjects that are more longterm as a basis for articles. You may well wish to include humorous items and you will certainly want pictures and eye-catching headlines. What about format? Tabloid or smaller?

All these general points can be discussed with a partner, especially if you have been working together on other parts of this book, but the final project must be an individual one if it is to be used for assessment in your coursework folder.

Loggerheads

Protecting tradition and ecology

The hideous cruelty of the hunt

Should the hunt be banned?

Stop the slaughter

THE NATIONAL TRUST has recently banned stag hunting on its land. About time! It's outrageous that anyone should be hunting stags in this day and age. It should have gone out in the dark ages.

Fox hunting should be got rid of too. It is a cruel activity that doesn't even deserve to be called a sport. Wild foxes, living peacefully in the countryside are hunted down by packs of dogs and aristocratic idiots in red coats.

The dogs are kept hungry so that they tear the fox to bits once caught. The foxes often leave behind young cubs, unable to fend for themselves.

It is uncivilised and barbaric. As Oscar Wilde quipped, it is "the unspeakable in pursuit of the uneatable".

Don't believe the hype

FOX HUNTING is one of the greatest spectacles of the English countryside. It is great sport that causes the minimum ammount of suffering to the fox.

The fox is a pest and farmers are pleased to see it got rid of. It is a scavenging and murderous animal: if it gets in a chicken pen it will kill every bird, not just the ones it wants to eat.

Hunting is also ecological. Vast areas of the countryside, and especially woodland are protected from development by people involved with the hunt.

Hunting is good exercise, good fun and good for the environment. The fox has a fair chance: most hunts end without a kill.

Leave the sport alone.

Horror of tortured children

CHILDREN around the world are being tortured every day — and cases of brutal treatment of young teenagers are increasing.

These are the shock findings of a special United Nations [UN] investigation team which has made a study of child abuse worldwide during the past 12 months. The group this week announced that countries such as the United Arab Emirates, Algeria, Chile, India and South Africa are among the worst offenders.

Their stunning comments come just weeks after 70 world leaders gathered at the UN headquarters in New York, in the United States, to pledge their support for action to help under-privileged youngsters everywhere.

Peter Koojimaans, the Dutch director of the investigation, accused 48 countries of using torture against young people. He claimed:

● Electric shocks were used in India to force children to confess to minor crimes.

● Children in the United Arab Emirates are often held in prison without being charged.

● Youngsters in Dubai regularly face severe beatings with a cane.

● Soldiers in Israel have committed offences against Palestinian children which are just too numerous to mention.

The report did recall one incident when a 15-year-old was dragged along the street by his hair then repeatedly beaten on the head with the soldiers' rifle butts.

But perhaps the worst cases of child abuse are committed in South Africa — where the authorities have often set light to their victims, and children detained under the Emergency Laws have suffered boiling water being poured down their backs.

You Tell Us

We asked you to tell us what your parents' most common 'sayings' are. Here are just a few:

"I don't care what everyone else wears, you're wearing this!"

"Turn off that nonsense I want to watch the news."

"Yes, I heard you the first twelve times."

AMAZING TRUE FACT

Sandwiches were invented by the Earl of Sandwich in the 18th century. He used to eat them when playing cards!

EVEN MORE AMAZING UNTRUE FACT

Sandwiches did not exist in the Middle Ages because knights in armour, with metal gauntlets, couldn't get the Clingfilm off them...

WHALING – A SCANDAL THAT CONTINUES

Most of the world has now agreed that killing whales is cruel and unnecessary. Several countries would like to resume whaling however, and so the further depletion of some species of whale remains a possibility.

The countries that continue whaling try to justify their actions in different ways. Some pretend that they have to keep numbers of whales down because the whales are eating too many fish. However, the opposite has been proved – that it is humans who are over-fishing the seas and threatening marine life. Another excuse some countries use is to pretend that they are killing whales for 'scientific' purposes. But the meat from these whales, usually ends up on sale in the fish market.

Whales and dolphins have been around for millions of years – much longer than humans. Yet there is a possibility that in your lifetime some species of whale might become extinct. And it is quite likely that particular groups or stocks of whales will die out in some areas of the world.

Even a whale's tail fluke (above) will be used to make whale based products which could be made from other things.

BRUCE COLEMAN LTD

The finished product

If you have access to a computer programme which will simulate newspaper layout, by all means use it. If not, you could type or word-process articles and do a 'paste-up' to produce the desired lay-out, adding headlines by hand. Or you could do it all in handwriting, of course.

Many of the sections you have already covered in this book will offer materials suitable for this final project. You could, for instance, include some of your funny poems (they appeal to all ages) and the fact sheet you wrote for the 'information' section might make a good article. The 'Campaign' unit on healthy eating might yield an article too.

If you prefer to submit all these earlier pieces separately in your folder, then you could make this final piece a *newsheet* on current events and topics in the news.

Either way, think about including a *letters* section in your magazine. This would give you a chance to demonstrate what you have learnt about the subjects that youngsters are interested in, by inventing typical letters from them. The Editor (you!) could reply.

Follow up

Many local newspapers run a 'Schools Page' which is farmed out to a different school each week for writing, editing and layout. If your local paper has one, why not contact the Editor and offer your services? You could use articles drawn from all your individual magazines and produce a whole page for them. If you can't find such a local scheme, you could write to the General Editor of the local paper and suggest she/he should give you a page for this purpose for one week. Most editors are grateful for any good material and very few would refuse such an offer if it were backed up with samples of the work you've done and an account of the research you have undertaken.

It would be very satisfying to see some of your work in print and you might be offered the chance to visit and learn more about the whole process of creating a newspaper.

Acknowledgements

We are grateful to the following for permission to reproduce copyright material:

Bushfield Community School for an extract from the *Bushfield Parent Guide*; Early Times, the national weekly newspaper for young people, for the article 'Horror of tortured children' from *Early Times* Issue 148, Nov. 15–21 1990; Ewan MacNaughton Associates for the feature 'You Tell Us' and article 'Whaling – a scandal that continues' from *The Young Telegraph* November 10 1990, © The Daily Telegraph plc/Young Telegraph; Faber & Faber Ltd for the poem 'Reading Scheme' from *Making Cocoa for Kingsley Amis* by Wendy Cope; the Controller of Her Majesty's Stationery Office for Sections 110–113 from *The Highway Code*; the Author's Agent for the poem 'First Day at School' by Roger McGough from *In The Glassroom* (Jonathan Cape Ltd); Spike Milligan Productions Ltd for the poems 'Mary Pugh' and 'Irish Stew' by Spike Milligan; Newspaper Publishing Plc/The Independent for the article 'Should the hunt be banned?' from *The Indy* November 15 1990; Thomas Nelson & Sons Ltd for the poems 'The Night Train' and 'Little Pig' from *Story Chest* (Shortland Publications, New Zealand); The Open University for an extract from *Open University Reading Development Course* Units 8/9 para. 2.22, p27; Random Century Group for an extract from *The Eighteenth Emergency* by Betsy Byars (The Bodley Head).

We are grateful to the following for permission to reproduce photographs:

Barnabys Picture Library, pages 33, 46 right, 47; Bus and Coach Council, page 38; Jonathan Cape Ltd for Quentin Blake's illustrations from Roald Dahl: *The Witches*, page 21; Counsel Ltd and H J Heinz, page 40; Daily Mail, page 16; Daily Telegraph plc, 1990 and Ewan MacNaughton Associates, pages 3 bottom, 46; Health Education Council for *What a Rotten Way to Treat your Teeth*, pages 3 centre, 36, 37 and *Your children's teeth*, page 39; William Heinemann for Janet and Allan Ahlberg: *Funny Bones*, pages 2 centre, 15; League against Cruel Sports, page 46 left; Mansell Collection, page 13; Spike Milligan Productions, page 27; Thomas Nelson and Sons Ltd for *National Writing Project*, pages 7, 8; Penguin Books, page 19; RSPCA, page 42; Ventura Publishing Ltd, page 10, from *Spot's First Walk*, published by William Heinemann Ltd, produced by Ventura Publishing Ltd, text and illustration c Eric Hill 1981; Geoff Ward, pages 2 top, 2 bottom, 3 top, 6, 24, 25, 31; Wella, page 42.

Cover illustration by Christopher Brown
Series designed by Jenny Portlock of Pentaprism

Longman Group UK Limited,
Longman House, Burnt Mill, Harlow,
Essex CM20 2JE, England
and Associated Companies throughout the world.

First published 1992

ISBN 0 582 07880 6

Produced by Longman Group (FE) Ltd
Printed in Hong Kong